# A JOURNEY THROUGH

## Music AND Memories

# RJ JOHNSON

Quantum
Discovery
A LITERARY AGENCY

A Journey Through Music and Memories
Copyright © 2024 by RJ Johnson

ISBN
978-1-964982-74-8 (Paperback)
978-1-964982-75-5 (eBook)
978-1-964982-73-1 (Hardcover)

*"Dedicated to my beloved wife, Linda, whose unwavering love and support have been the true guiding light of my life. Her presence is the heart of this journey, and every step I take is a reflection of the strength and inspiration she has given me."*

# *Table of Contents*

*"A journey through life is nothing without love and dreams!"*

# FOREWORD

I'm certain I cannot do justice in fully capturing the character of this remarkable gentleman!

I've had the pleasure of knowing Mr. Johnson for many years. His extraordinary talent in singing, guitar playing, and songwriting is truly beyond words. I believe now is the perfect time to share his work with the world. This book is a heartfelt journey, reflecting his lifelong love and passion for the music industry.

A word of caution: this book will stir every emotion you have! So, sit back, buckle up, and enjoy the ride!

Sincerely,

Thomas Theophilus

~ Author and Poet ~

# PREFACE

*"After enduring years of soaring highs,*
*crushing lows,*
*and heart-wrenching heartbreaks,*
*with fleeting moments of joy scattered in between,*
*it's those glimmers of hope*
*and happiness that make the entire journey of life*
*truly meaningful and unforgettable."*

# ACKNOWLEDGMENTS

*"My beloved wife, who has stood by my side
through every challenge and triumph over the years,
has been my unwavering source of strength
and the true inspiration behind this book.
Her love, support, and belief in me have fueled my journey
and made this story possible."*

# INTRODUCTION

*"A deeply heartfelt journey that reflects
a life transformed through countless changes,
exploring the reasons behind them,
and revealing the emotional tale of enduring love.
This story captures the essence of true love
and the profound experiences that shape one's path,
offering a glimpse into the resilience of the human heart."*

# BABY PLEASE COME BACK HOME

*I'M WRITING THIS LETTER DARLING,*
*HOPING THAT YOU WILL*
*REPLY*
*MAYBE YOU'LL FIND YOU STILL LOVE ME*
*AND THEN I WON'T HAVE TO CRY*

*BABY PLEASE COME BACK TO ME, LET'S START ALL OVER*
*AGAIN*
*I PROMISE THAT I WILL BE TRUE FOR EVER MORE*
*BABY PLEASE COME BACK HOME*

*I KNOW I'VE BEEN BAD IN THE PAST DEAR*
*TREATING YOU LIKE YOU WERE DIRT*
*AND NOW THAT I REALIZE YOU'VE GONE*
*BABY DON'T THINK IT DON'T HURT*

*BABY PLEASE COME BACK TO ME, LET'S START ALL OVER*
*AGAIN*
*I PROMISE THAT I WILL BE TRUE FOR EVER MORE*
*BABY PLEASE COME BACK HOME*

*I KNOW I'VE BEEN BAD IN THE PAST DEAR*
*TREATING YOU LIKE YOU WERE DIRT*
*AND NOW THAT I REALIZE YOU'VE GONE*
*BABY DON'T THINK IT DON'T HURT*

BABY PLEASE COME BACK TO ME, LET'S START ALL OVER
*AGAIN*
*I PROMISE THAT I WILL BE TRUE FOR EVER MORE*
*BABY PLEASE COME BACK HOME*

# Chapter 1

## Baby Please Come Back Home

When my wife embarked on her recent trip—though the destination escapes me now—I was left to navigate the intricacies of managing our household alone. The seemingly simple tasks that she effortlessly handles, from washing the dishes to sweeping and vacuuming the floors, feeding the dog, and keeping everything in order, suddenly became monumental challenges for me. What I had once viewed as routine chores quickly transformed into an exhausting marathon. I was continually struggling to keep up with the responsibilities that had always been her domain.

The absence of her presence was profoundly felt. The house, usually filled with the soothing hum of her activities and her gentle voice, felt eerily quiet and still. I noticed every small detail she attends to—the way she arranges the cushions, the aroma of her cooking, and the subtle, comforting patterns she creates in our daily lives. Without her, the house felt like a hollow shell, and I was painfully aware of the emptiness left in her wake. The usual rhythm of our home was disrupted, and the silence seemed to amplify the void of her presence.

As the days wore on, my thoughts began to drift towards a more distressing possibility: what if she decided to leave me permanently? The notion was more than just unsettling; it was an emotional avalanche. I found myself overwhelmed by the thought of facing a future without her, grappling with the idea of waking up to a life devoid of her laughter, her touch, and her unwavering support. The mundane tasks that once seemed trivial now felt insurmountable without her by my side. The house would be a constant reminder of her absence, a stark, cold space where every corner would echo with the memory of her warmth and love.

The emotional weight of this realization became almost unbearable. I understood that her role in my life goes far beyond the practicalities of daily living. She is the heart of our home, the source of my joy and stability. Her presence enriches every moment of my life, and the thought of losing her brought a profound sense of dread and helplessness. The more I contemplated this possibility, the more I came to appreciate just how deeply intertwined our lives are.

In an attempt to process these intense emotions and express the depth of my feelings, I turned to songwriting. The song that emerged from this experience is a heartfelt tribute to the fear and sorrow of losing her. Through its lyrics, I aimed to capture the profound sense of loss and the emotional void that her departure would create. The song is a reflection of the nightmare that such a loss would be—a raw, unfiltered portrayal of the emptiness and heartache I would face without her.

This song is not merely a musical composition; it is a testament to the immeasurable value she brings into my life. It represents my deepest fears and my overwhelming gratitude for the life we share. It is a reminder of how irreplaceable she is and how much I cherish every moment we have together. Through this song, I hope to convey the depth of my love and the vital role she plays in my world, offering a glimpse into the emotional turmoil I experienced and the profound appreciation I have for her presence in my life.

# HEY LITTLE GIRL

*HEY LITTLE GIRL, DON'T YOU WALK OUT ON ME*
*WHEN I'M ALONE. I THINK OF YOU*
*HEY LITTLE GIRL, WANT YOU SAY YOU'RE MINE*
*THEN I'LL KNOW FOR SURE, YES I WILL*

*YES I WILL. YES I WILL, YES I WILL, YES I WILL*

*SO MUCH TIME HAS GONE BY SINCE*
*YOU LEFT THAT NIGHT*
*AND YOUR KISS TO ME, MADE ME FEEL SO RIGHT*
*I WANT YOU SO, BUT YOU ARE FAR AWAY*
*MY HEART LONGS FOR YOU EVERY NIGHT AND EVERY DAY*

*YES IT DOES, YES IT DOES, YES IT DOES. YES IT DOES*

*GIVE ME ONE LAST CHANCE, TO GET YOU BACK MY DEAR*
*I LOVE YOU SO, BUT YOU ARE NEVER HERE*
*ONE MORE TIME, JUST KISS MY LIPS*
*THEN I'LL KNOW FOR SURE. YES I WILL*

*YES I WILL. YES I WILL, YES I WILL, YES I WILL*

# Chapter 2

## Hey Little Girl

During my teenage years, my cousin Don and I were more than just family; we were kindred spirits and creative collaborators. We spent countless hours together, dreaming up melodies and lyrics that reflected our youthful ambitions and shared experiences. One of our most cherished projects was a song that we started writing together. Don, with his natural talent and flair for music, composed the melodies that captured our hearts, while I contributed lyrics that expressed our collective vision.

Our collaboration was more than a musical endeavor; it was a reflection of our deep bond and the joy we found in each other's company. We envisioned this song as a testament to our friendship and a symbol of our dreams. But just as we were on the verge of completing it, tragedy struck. Don's unexpected passing was a shattering blow. His death left a void in my life that was impossible to fill, and the unfinished song became a bittersweet reminder of the dreams we had yet to realize.

In the wake of Don's death, the song was set aside, buried beneath the weight of grief and loss. The melodies we had crafted together and the potential of our project were overshadowed by the profound sense of emptiness left by his absence. Years went by, and the pain of losing Don became a part of my life's landscape, though it never truly faded.

It wasn't until I began reconnecting with my love for songwriting that I stumbled upon the remnants of our old project. The melodies Don had composed and the incomplete lyrics stirred a powerful wave of nostalgia and resolve within me. I realized that this song was more than just unfinished music; it was a piece of our shared history and a tribute to Don's legacy.

With renewed determination, I set out to complete the song, not just as an act of creative closure but as a heartfelt homage to Don. The lyrics I crafted were deeply personal, reflecting a chapter of Don's life that had been significant to him—his relationship with his girlfriend. The song tells the story of their struggles and the heartbreak of a love that couldn't endure. Through these lyrics, I aimed to capture the essence of their relationship and the pain of unresolved emotions that Don experienced.

Completing the song was a deeply emotional journey. It allowed me to reconnect with Don's spirit and honor the bond we shared. Each line of the song is imbued with memories of our time together, the joy of our creative partnership, and the sorrow of his absence. It is a tribute to the impact he had on my life and a way to keep his memory alive.

This song is dedicated to Don—a lasting testament to our friendship, his musical talent, and the love we shared for creating something beautiful together. Through these lyrics, I hope to celebrate his memory and ensure that his legacy endures. It stands as a powerful reminder of the special connection we had and the dreams we pursued together, a legacy of love and creativity that will forever be cherished in my heart.

# I HAVE YOU

*I'VE GOT THE WORLD IN MY HAND, I'M A HAPPY MAN*
*NOW I KNOW WHAT A LOVE CAN BE*
*BEFORE I THOUGHT MY LIFE WAS THROUGH*
*THEN I FELL IN LOVE WITH YOU*
*NOW I REALIZE WHAAT A LOVE CAN BE*

*I HAVE YOU TO CALL ME DARLING*
*I HAVE YOU TO HOLD ME CLOSE*
*AND EVERYTIME I SEE YOU, IT'S YOU I LOVE THE MOST*

*YOU MAY WONDER WHY I'M HAPPY*
*I'VE GOT A RIGHT TO BE*
*IT'S NOT EVERY DAY A FELLOW FALLS IN LOVE LIKE ME*
*I SEARCHED THE WORLD ALL OVER,*
*THOUGHT I WOULD NEVER*
*SEE*
*THE THING I WANTED MOST IN LIFE,*
*HAS FOUND IT'S WAY TO ME*

*I HAVE YOU TO CALL ME DARLING*
*I HAVE YOU TO HOLD ME CLOSE*
*AND EVERYTIME I SEE YOU, IT'S YOU I LOVE THE MOST*

*YOU MAY WONDER WHY I'M HAPPY*
*I'VE GOT A RIGHT TO BE*

# Chapter 3

*I Have You*

This song is a deeply personal tribute to my wife, who has been my unwavering support through life's many trials. Over the years, I've dedicated myself to building a successful career, striving to create a comfortable life for us. Despite my best efforts, the journey has often been fraught with challenges and setbacks. There have been times when the weight of repeated failures felt almost unbearable, leaving me grappling with feelings of inadequacy and despair.

In those moments of struggle, when the walls seem to close in and hope feels out of reach, there is one profound constant that anchors me: my wife. Her presence in my life is a beacon of light, cutting through the darkness of my self-doubt and offering a sense of stability amidst the chaos. When everything else seems to be falling apart, it is the thought of her—her strength, her love, and her unwavering belief in me—that provides comfort and a glimmer of hope.

The idea for this song emerged on one of those particularly dark days. As I faced yet another wave of disappointment and felt as though my efforts had amounted to little, I found myself overwhelmed by a deep sense of hopelessness. But even in the midst of this emotional storm, the realization that I had her in my life struck me with a powerful clarity. It was in that moment of profound struggle that the title "I Have You" was born, symbolizing the solace and strength I derive from her support.

The song's lyrics are a heartfelt reflection of this realization. They capture the essence of the comfort and reassurance she provides during times of hardship. Each line is infused with gratitude for her steadfast presence and the way she lifts me up when I am at my lowest. Her love is a refuge from the storms of life, a reminder that no matter how difficult the path may be, having her by my side makes every challenge more bearable.

The process of writing this song was both cathartic and enlightening. It allowed me to channel my feelings of despair into something beautiful and meaningful. The song is not just a personal expression but also a celebration of the profound impact she has on my life. It stands as a testament to the power of love and the incredible strength it provides in the face of adversity.

Through this song, I hope to convey the depth of my appreciation for her and the vital role she plays in my journey. It is a reminder that even when the world feels overwhelming and hope seems distant, the love and support of someone special can make all the difference. "I Have You" is a tribute to her and a celebration of the unbreakable bond we share—a beacon of hope and a source of strength in times of darkness.

# NOW THAT YOU'RE GONE

*NOW THAT YOU'RE GONE, LEFT ME HERE ALL ALONE*
*AND NOW I REALIZE, WHAT A FOOL I MUST HAVE BEEN*
*LEAVING YOU ALL ALONE,*

*SO MANY NIGHTS AWAY FROM HOME*
*SINCE I HAD YOU ON THE PHONE,*

*I'D THOUGHT I ASK IF YOU'LL COME HOME*

*I KNOW THAT I HAVE TREATED YOU SO BAD*
*BUT IF YOU PROMISE YOU'LL FORGIVE ME,*

*I PROMISE I'LL BE TRUE*
*WHY CAN'T YOU SEE, WHAT YOU'RE DOING TO ME*
*SINCE I HAD YOU ON THE PHONE,*

*I'D THOUGHT I ASK IF YOU'LL COME HOME*
*I KNOW THAT I HAVE TREATED YOU SO BAD*
*BUT IF YOU PROMISE YOU'LL FORGIVE ME,*

*I PROMISE I'LL BE TRUE*
*WHY CAN'T YOU SEE, WHAT YOU'RE DOING TO ME*
*SINCE I HAD YOU ON THE PHONE,*

*I'D THOUGHT I ASK IF YOU'LL COME HOME*

# Chapter 4

## *Now That You're Gone*

Back in the day, I was on the road constantly, working as a traveling salesman. It seemed like I was always on the move—living out of suitcases, staying in motels, and watching the days blur together. Meanwhile, Linda was back home, holding down the fort by herself. I'd call her every evening, no matter where I was, just to hear her voice and make sure everything was okay. But as time went on, those calls became more than just routine. They were a lifeline, a connection to the one person who kept me grounded amid all the hustle.

It was during those long stretches away from home that doubt and fear started to creep in. I began asking myself tough questions: What if Linda got tired of being alone so much? What if she reached her breaking point and decided enough was enough? The thought of coming home one day and finding an empty house shook me to my core. The more I thought about it, the more it ate away at me. My mind would go down dark paths, imagining a future without her in it—a future I knew I couldn't handle.

I'd lie awake in those lonely motel rooms, staring at the ceiling, with those fears turning into vivid nightmares. In those dreams, I'd walk into our house, call out her name, and be met with silence. I'd feel the emptiness, the loss, and the heartache of a life without the person who meant everything to me. I realized that the life I was leading wasn't just hard on me—it was hard on her too. The distance wasn't just physical; it was starting to become emotional as well.

One particularly sleepless night, I grabbed a pen and paper and began pouring all those swirling thoughts and emotions into a song. Writing was my way of processing the fear, the love, and the desperate need to hold on to what truly mattered. The song became a reflection of everything I was going through—the worry, the regret, and the realization that I might be losing something priceless if I didn't make a change.

After that night, I couldn't shake the feeling that I was heading down the wrong path. I took a long, hard look at my life and decided that no job was worth risking my marriage. I handed in my resignation and walked away from a stable career, choosing instead to be at home with Linda every day. It wasn't an easy decision, but it was the right one. The relief I felt was immediate, and the joy of being home with her far outweighed any of the sacrifices we had to make.

Looking back now, I realize how close I came to losing the love of my life, all because I was too focused on work. That song, *Now That You're Gone,* became a reminder of the choices I made and how lucky I am that I didn't let fear become a reality. Every time I play it, I'm reminded of how love and commitment pulled us through—and how grateful I am that Linda was still there when I finally came home for good.

# THE CHICKEN SNAKE BOOGIE

*WELL I WAS WALKING THROUGH THE MEADOW*
*WHERE THE GREEN GRASS GROWS*

*I DIDN'T HAVE NO SOCKS OR NO SHOES ON MY TOES*

*I STEPPED ON SOMETHING AND IT STARTED TO SHAKE*
*I KNEW RIGHT THEN I HAD STEPPED ON A SNAKE*
*I GOT THE CHICKEN SNAKE BOOGIE, I*
*SAID THE CHICKEN SNAKE BOOGIE*
*I GOT THE CHICKEN SNAKE BOOGIE AND*
*IT'S CRAWLING ALL OVER ME*

*WELL I JUMPED UP AND I STARTED TO RUN*
*I WAS GOING HOME JUST TO GET MY GUN*
*I JUMPED THE CREEK AND WHAT DID I SEE*
*THAT SNAKE IN FRONT JUST LAUGHING AT ME*

*I GOT THE CHICKEN SNAKE BOOGIE, I*
*SAID THE CHICKEN SNAKE BOOGIE*

*I GOT THE CHICKEN SNAKE BOOGIE AND*
*IT'S CRAWLING ALL OVER ME*

*WHEN I GOT HOME I WENT AND GRABBED MY HOE*
*I MISSED THAT SNAKE AND I CHOPPED MY TOE*
*I HIT HIM ONCE MORE AND I MISSED HIS HEAD*
*I KNEW RIGHT THEN THAT SNAKE WON'T DEAD*
*I GOT THE CHICKEN SNAKE BOOGIE, I*
*SAID THE CHICKEN SNAKE BOOGIE*
*I GOT THE CHICKEN SNAKE BOOGIE AND*
*IT'S CRAWLING ALL OVER ME*

# Chapter 5

## *The Chicken Snake Boogie*

This song is rooted in a real experience from my days working on the farm, and it's a tale I'll never forget. It all happened one sweltering summer afternoon in Johnston County, NC, when I was out in the tobacco fields helping my grandfather with the harvest. The sun was blazing, and the air was thick with that sticky Southern humidity. We had been out there all day, sweating under the weight of the work, but little did I know, the most memorable moment of the day was about to unfold.

I was making my way down one of the rows, lost in the rhythm of the task, when suddenly I felt something squishy and slick under my boot. At first, I thought it was just mud or a thick root, but when I looked down, my heart nearly stopped. Wrapped beneath my foot was the biggest, meanest chicken snake I'd ever laid eyes on! It was as thick as a tree branch and stretched out like a shadow in the blazing sun.

Instinct took over, and before I knew it, I was airborne, jumping straight up like I had springs in my legs. I took off running like my life depended on it, making a beeline for the barn. But in the middle of my mad dash, I glanced over my shoulder and couldn't believe what I saw—this snake wasn't letting me go that easy! It was hot on my heels, slithering like it had some kind of vendetta against me.

Now, growing up in the country, I'd learned that when it came to snakes, you didn't mess around—you grabbed the nearest garden hoe and went to work. So, with the snake gaining on me, I desperately scanned the ground for a hoe or anything I could use as a weapon. Just as the snake was closing in, I spotted one leaning against the barn wall. I snatched it up, turned around, and started swinging like I was in the World Series! I was hacking and chopping with all my might, but in my panic, I wasn't exactly aiming too well. I came within a hair's breadth of slicing my own toes clean off as I tried to deal with that stubborn snake!

After what felt like a lifetime, I finally managed to land a solid hit. The snake curled up and slithered away, but I was still shaking from the adrenaline. Once the dust settled and my heart rate slowed down a bit, I couldn't help but chuckle at how ridiculous the whole scene must've looked. There I was, a grown man running from a snake, flailing a hoe around like a madman, and almost chopping off my own feet in the process!

That's when it hit me—this wild, backwoods experience was too good not to turn into a song. There was rhythm in the chase, a beat in the panic, and a tune in the thrill of the moment. I started humming a little melody right then and there, and before long, "The Chicken Snake Boogie" was born.

This song is a foot-stomping, good-time tune that takes you right back to that summer day in the fields. It's got a little humor, a lot of energy, and a whole lot of country spirit. It's more than just a story about a snake; it's a slice of rural life, a reminder of the simple days, and a tribute to the unpredictable adventures that come with working the land. Every time I play it, I'm transported back to that row of tobacco, the sun beating down, and that slithering snake giving me the scare of a lifetime. But most of all, it's a reminder that even in the most unexpected, nerve-wracking moments, there's always a bit of music to be found.

# THE WOMAN I CALL DARLING

*WHEN I LOOK DOWN AT THE RING ON MY FINGER*
*I WONDER WHO WOULD HAVE A MAN LIKE ME*
*THEN I THINK ABOUT THE WOMAN I CALL DARLING*
*AND I LOOK UP AND MY WIFE SMILES AT ME*

*SHE MADE ME WHAT I AM*
*AND I AM HAPPY*
*SHE GAVE ME ALL HER LOVE*
*AND SO MUCH MORE*
*I OWE MY LIFE TO THIS WOMAN I*
*CALL DARLING*
*AND THAT'S EXACTLY WHAT I GAVE TO HER*

*SOMETIMES AGO I WANDERED*
*DOWN THE STREETS OF TOWN*
*I WAS DRUNK, SO BLIND I COULDN'T SEE*
*THAT'S WHEN I MET THIS WOMAN I CALL DARLING*
*SHE TOOK ME IN AND MADE A MAN OF ME*

*SHE MADE ME WHAT I AM*
*AND I AM HAPPY*
*SHE GAVE ME ALL HER LOVE*
*AND SO MUCH MORE*
*I OWE MY LIFE TO THIS WOMAN I*
*CALL DARLING*
*AND THAT'S EXACTLY WHAT I GAVE TO HER*

# Chapter 6

## *The Woman I Call Darling*

This song is a deeply personal tribute to my wife, Linda, who has been my constant source of love and strength throughout the years. Our journey together hasn't always been easy—like every couple, we've faced our share of challenges, uncertainties, and tough times. But through it all, Linda has remained my rock, my guiding light, and the love of my life.

From the very beginning, Linda showed me what true love and devotion really mean. There have been moments when I doubted myself, when life's pressures weighed me down, and when I felt like I was falling short in everything I tried to do. But Linda never wavered. She stood by me with an unwavering belief that I could overcome any obstacle, no matter how tough things got. Her faith in me has been a lifeline, pulling me through the darkest days.

I remember times when I struggled to make ends meet, feeling like every effort was met with failure. It's easy to be supportive when everything is going well, but Linda's support never depended on circumstances. Whether I was at my best or my worst, she was there, cheering me on, offering a shoulder to lean on, and always making sure I knew she was in my corner. She's the kind of woman who can lift you up with just a smile, reminding you that love isn't about success or perfection—it's about being there for each other, no matter what.

There's a kind of quiet strength in Linda that has always inspired me. She has a way of seeing the good in every situation and finding hope even when things seem bleak. When I was ready to throw in the towel, she would gently remind me that setbacks are temporary and that we could face anything together. Her love gave me the courage to keep going, to keep trying, and to believe in myself when I felt like I had nothing left to give.

It's because of her that I've been able to grow, learn, and keep pursuing my dreams. She has accepted me fully for who I am, flaws and all, without ever asking for anything in return except love. I know I owe so much of who I am today to her support, patience, and unwavering belief in me. That's why I say in the song, "I owe her my life," because it's the truth—without her, I wouldn't be the man I am today.

When I sat down to write this song, I wanted it to be a reflection of everything she has meant to me over the years. "The Woman I Call Darling" is more than just a term of endearment; it's a title she's earned through years of love, sacrifice, and loyalty. Every note, every lyric, is a piece of our story—the story of a woman who has loved unconditionally, supported endlessly, and believed wholeheartedly in the power of us.

This song is my way of expressing the gratitude I feel for her every single day. It's a reminder of the love we share, the bond we've built, and the life we've created together. Linda is more than just my wife; she's my best friend, my partner, and the love of my life. She truly is, and always will be, "The Woman I Call Darling."

# Chapter 7

## A Journey to Music and Memories

From as early as I can remember, music has been a deeply ingrained and cherished part of my life. My journey with music began in the comforting, sacred environment of the church, where the hymns sung each Sunday provided a serene backdrop to my early experiences. This initial spark was further ignited by my fascination with the iconic sounds of Hank Williams Sr. and Elvis Presley, whose music resonated with me on a profound level. My cousin Don, who was the same age as me, received his first guitar at the tender age of ten. The moment I saw him with that guitar, I was filled with an unshakable desire to learn to play it myself.

When Don received a new guitar, my parents, recognizing my burgeoning interest, bought his old Silver-tone from Sears for me. This old guitar, with its worn fretboard and distinctive tone, became my refuge and sanctuary. I would spend countless hours after school strumming away, the sounds echoing through the house. My relentless practice soon became a bit of an ordeal for my parents, leading them to send me to the outhouse in the backyard to spare their ears. (For those unfamiliar, an outhouse is a simple, outdoor toilet, a remnant of a simpler era.)

Despite the challenges, my dedication to music did not waver. As I immersed myself in playing, my skills gradually improved. The music that once sounded chaotic began to flow more naturally, and I ventured into singing along. My mother, ever supportive and enthusiastic, encouraged me to perform publicly. I was soon standing in front of the church congregation, nervously but proudly singing "I Never Knew You"– my very first public performance.

That moment was pivotal; it was then that I realized music was not just a hobby, but my true calling. Equipped with only three basic chords and a Mel Bay beginner's guitar book, I set out on a path of self-teaching and discovery.

As time went on, I upgraded to a newer guitar from Roses Dime Store, a significant milestone that marked a new chapter in my musical journey. I continued to play alongside Don Pittman and another cousin, Royce Lamn, forming a band we named "The Tobacco Trail Trio." We took every opportunity to perform, from local community events to small gigs, and we developed a reputation for our lively and engaging performances. Even when our paths eventually diverged, my passion for music remained undiminished.

High school brought new opportunities for growth and creativity. Alongside a fellow student, Connie Owens, I participated in a school talent show where I debuted my first original song, "Soldier Boy." The song, deeply influenced by the turmoil of the Vietnam War, told the heart-wrenching story of a young couple whose wedding was postponed when the groom was drafted. After suffering wounds in battle, the groom was presumed dead, and his girlfriend, believing him lost, married his best friend. When he returned and discovered this betrayal, he chose to leave, never to return. The emotional depth of the song resonated deeply with those who heard it, and it marked the beginning of my songwriting career.

After graduation, I enlisted in the Army National Guard but was discharged before completing boot camp. Undeterred, I returned home with a renewed focus on my music. During this time, I met Rick, a talented guitarist and close friend. I taught him how to play, and together we formed "Randy Johnson and the Young Countrymen." We recorded an album featuring my original songs and performed extensively, building a dedicated following and gaining valuable experience.

Our musical journey continued with the formation of a new group called "Sunshine," which included Rick, his wife Jane, and my first wife. We performed across various venues, including restaurants, malls, and local events. We modeled our style after the harmonious sound of groups like "Dave and Sugar," and we developed a unique four-part harmony that set us apart. Our collaboration with another band, "Showdown," led to a memorable performance at Busch Gardens in Virginia. We competed in the Battle of the Bands and won the prestigious Ginny Award, presented by Nashville Music. A particularly exciting highlight was our appearance on the national TV show "You Can Be a Star" on The Nashville Network. Backed by the Bill Anderson Band, we performed songs by Charlie Pride and Ricky Nelson, an experience that stands out as a peak in our musical career.

As the years went by, our musical pursuits evolved, and we formed "Some Assembly Required." This group was known for its eclectic and diverse range of music, covering everything from classic country to contemporary hits. Our performances took us to new and varied audiences, reflecting our versatility and passion for music. Each performance was a testament to our enduring love for music, and our repertoire grew to include a wide array of genres and styles.

Today, I play and sing exclusively in church, where my music has found a new and deeply meaningful purpose. Looking back on those vibrant years of performances, creative exploration, and heartfelt connections, I hold those memories close to my heart. The joy of making music and sharing it with others continues to be an integral part of who I am. The highs and lows of my musical journey have left an indelible mark on my soul, and those formative experiences continue to shape my life and my art.

www.ingramcontent.com/pod-product-compliance
Lightning Source LLC
Chambersburg PA
CBHW051651120626
46551CB00015B/2308